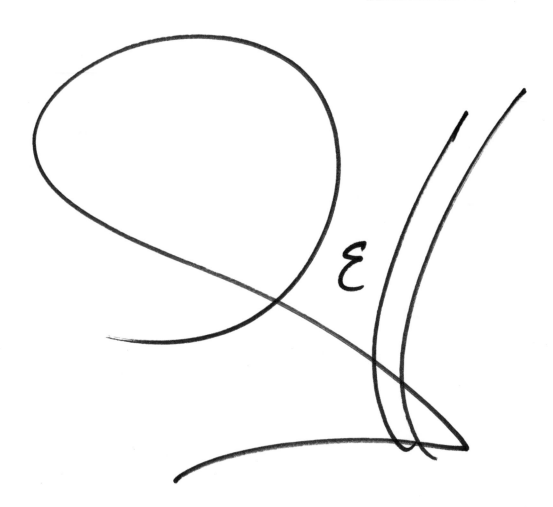

3

LIVING UP TO YOUR EULOGY

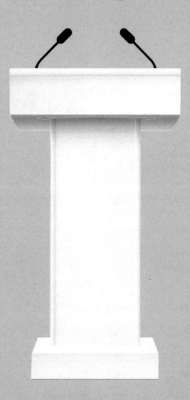

Inspirational Stories and Quotations to Encourage You
to Live a Life That Will Be Lovingly Remembered

Jeff Drew
with Stuart Clark and Dave Clark

LIVING UP TO YOUR EULOGY

Inspirational Stories and Quotations to Encourage You to Live a Life That Will Be Lovingly Remembered

Jeffrey Drew, Stuart Clark and Dave Clark

Bodley Creations, LLC

Published by Bodley Creations, LLC, St. Louis, MO, BodleyCreations.com

Copyright © 2021 by Jeffrey Drew, Stuart Clark and Dave Clark

To order copies or for more information on Living Up to Your Eulogy. Visit our website at:www.bodleycreations.com

Cover Design: Tricia Martin

Project Management and Interior design: Davis Creative Publishing Partners, DavisCreative.com

Library of Congress Cataloging-in-Publication Data

Library of Congress Control Number: 2020952556

Jeffrey Drew, Stuart Clark and Dave Clark

LIVING UP TO YOUR EULOGY

Inspirational Stories and Quotations to Encourage You to Live a Life That Will Be Lovingly Remembered

ISBN: 978-0-578-82631-8 (hardback)
    978-1-7372462-0-6 (paperback)
    978-1-7372462-1-3 (ebook)

BISAC Subject headings:

    1. OCC019000 BODY, MIND & SPIRIT/Inspiration & Personal Growth   2. SEL021000 SELF-HELP/ Motivational & Inspirational   3. FAM054000 FAMILY & RELATIONSHIPS/Life Stages / Mid-Life

    2021

ATTENTION CORPORATIONS, UNIVERSITIES, COLLEGES AND PROFESSIONAL ORGANIZATIONS: Quantity discounts are available on bulk purchases of this book for educational, gift purposes, or as premiums for increasing magazine subscriptions or renewals. Special books or book excerpts can also be created to fit specific needs. For information, please contact Bodley Creations, bodleycreations.com@gmail.com.

Dedications

My brother Buck put it so well, the three of us Drew boys were born on third base. We were so "blessed" to have parents like Charlie and Pat. I feel the very same way about both my brothers, Buck and John.

– Jeff

To my beautiful wife, Ann. Thank you for absolutely everything you have given me. I will always love you.

– Stuart

To my amazing wife, Margaret. I will be eternally grateful for your love, your kindness and your incredible heart.

– Dave

Table of Contents

Forward

In early January 2021, I started feeling sick with flu-like symptoms. I tried to nurse myself back to health taking various medications. After several days, my condition continued to rapidly worsen. My girlfriend called me the morning of January 8th and noticed that my breathing was very labored. She said she was coming over and insisted she take me to the emergency room at the nearest hospital. Come to find out I had COVID pneumonia which had ravaged my lung capacity and I was placed in ICU. The doctor who examined me later told me that if I had waited another day coming to the hospital, I probably would have died.

I feel that I've been given a new lease on life and now I want to become a better version of myself. Two areas of my life stand out the most in what I must do differently than before.

Be more grateful.

How often do we truly stop to think about what we have? Every day now, I take a moment to thank God I'm alive and to try to appreciate more the things I've taken for granted in the past.

Be more kind.

The importance of kindness was heightened for me during and after my stay at the hospital. From opening the door for someone to donating to a worthy charity to visiting a nursing home, we can make life better and easier for others.

I hope that my story here and words on the pages that follow can inspire you to do more for others. Your life is your message to the world. Make sure it's inspiring.

– Jeff Drew

Introduction

You are going to die.

There is nothing that is more certain than your death. And It may happen a lot sooner to you than you are expecting. Why, it could even be this very day.

We all realize we are going to die. So why then do we live our lives as though there's always going to be another tomorrow?

The further down the road we go, the funerals we attend seem to move us more and more. We're drawn to the eulogies because listening to friends and loved ones stand up and tell glowing stories about the dearly departed often causes us to wonder.

The eulogist at a funeral always describes the deceased as a person of high integrity and character. As we listen, sometimes we have to ponder if the eulogist's kind words are genuinely felt or are they just said out of respect for the departed. We have heard many eulogies that we feel confident in saying that not only the eulogist, but also most of the people in attendance knew that the laudatory words for the deceased were far from the actual truth.

We wonder if the nice things said about us at our funerals will be heartfelt and true. Did we really live the kind of life where we made a difference? Did we impact lives in a meaningful way? Were our lives well lived? Will people remember us, five…ten…even twenty years after we leave this Earth?

It's not too late to make a positive change in our lives. Begin today. Start small and just take the first step, doing kindhearted deeds on a daily basis that make a positive impact on other people.

Our book presents stories, excerpts, quotes and images…hopefully inspirational ones that can help guide you to living a life that makes a difference…a life where it's possible to live up to your eulogy.

– Dave Clark

Advice to Live By

Journalist David Brooks, in his 2014 speech at the TED (Technology, Entertainment and Design) Conference, talked about the resume virtues versus the eulogy virtues. In his speech, he asks the simple question, "Should we live for our eulogy or our resume?"

"For most of us, the answer is simple. We want to be remembered as someone who spent time with friends and family, as someone who loved and was loved, and as someone who made a difference beyond their career in the lives of those around them."

"What's a good investment?

Go home from work early and spend the afternoon throwing a ball around with your son."

– Ben Stein, American writer, commentator

Thousands of men breathe, move, and live, pass off the stage of life, and are heard of no more. Why?

They did not partake of good, and none in the world were blessed by them. None could point to them as the guide to their redemption. They wrote nothing, not a word they said could be recalled. And so they passed on: their light went out in darkness, and they were not remembered more than insects of yesterday.

Will you thus live and die, O man immortal? Live for something. Do good, and leave behind you a monument of virtue that the storm of time can never destroy. Write your name, in kindness, love, and mercy, on the hearts of thousands you come in contact with year by year: you will never be forgotten.

No! Your name, your deeds, will be as legible on the hearts you leave behind you as the stars on the brow of evening. Good deeds will shine as the stars of heaven.

– Dr. Thomas Chalmers, theologian

"How am I living?"

Rick Rigsby delivered a very moving and inspirational commencement speech at Cal Maritime University in 2017. His speech was about the wisest person he ever met...a third grade dropout. That third grade dropout happened to be his father.

His father dropped out of school to help out on the family farm. He taught himself how to read and write and became a "simple cook." "He challenged himself to be the best that he could all the days of his life." Rick stated that he has four degrees. His brother is a judge. But, Rick emphatically maintained that their father was the smartest one in the family.

Some of his father's most memorable words of wisdom…

"I won't have a problem if you aim high and miss, but I'm gonna have a real issue if you aim low and hit."

"Son, you'd rather be an hour early than a minute late."

My mother said, for nearly 30 years, my father left the house at 3:45 in the morning. One day, she asked him why. He said, "Maybe one of my boys will catch me in the act of excellence."

The one question that his father asked his son every day…"How are you living?"

Rick says that his father would suggest that you live life as follows…

- Don't judge.

- Show up early.

- Be kind.

- If you're going to do something, do it the right way.

- It's never wrong to do the right thing.

- How you do anything is how you do everything, and in that way, you will grow your influence to make an impact. In that way, you will honor all those who have gone before you and who have invested in you.

- Look in those unlikeliest places for wisdom.

And ask yourself every night, "How am I living?

"Resolve to be tender with the young, compassionate with the aged, sympathetic with the striving, and tolerant with the weak and wrong. Sometime in life you will have been all of these.

– Dr. Robert H. Goodard,
American engineer, professor

Two excerpts from Billy Crystal's book, *Still Foolin' 'Em: Where I've Been, Where I'm Going, and Where the Hell Are My Keys.*

"The inevitable becomes clearer every day. Sometimes like a sudden rainstorm, I get that scared, sad feeling that time is getting shorter. The dark part of my imagination overwhelms me, and I picture myself old and feeble. I can't stop conjuring the saddest images my mind can muster, and I'm lost—and then I hear the footsteps running toward me and I hear the giggles, and they yell "Grandpa!" and suddenly they're in my arms and I squeeze them and hold on to them for dear life, and that's a very accurate statement. It's a dear life. One that I get to share with them while I watch them grow and help get them ready for what's to come."

On his Uncle Berns dying…

"I just started sobbing and saying thank you. Thank you for your love, your inspiration, your support, your guidance, your laughter. When I ran out of thank-yous, I finally said goodbye."

"Let us live so that when we come to die even the undertaker will be sorry."

– Mark Twain, American author

"If you want others to be happy, practice compassion. If you want to be happy, practice compassion."

– The Dalai Lama

A Little Fellow Follows Me

A careful man I ought to be,
A little fellow follows me.
I dare not go astray,
For fear he'll go the self-same way.

I cannot once escape his eyes,
Whatever he sees me do, he tries.
Like me, he says, he's going to be,
The little boy who follows me.

He thinks that I am good and fine,
Believes in every word of mine.
The base in me he must not see,
That little fellow who follows me.

I must remember as I go,
Thru summers' sun and winters' snow.
I am building for the years to be,
In the little boy who follows me.

by Rev. Claude Wisdom White, Sr

"People are often unreasonable, irrational, and self-centered.
Forgive them anyway.

If you are kind, people may accuse you of selfish, ulterior motives.
Be kind anyway.

If you are successful, you will win some unfaithful friends and some genuine enemies.
Succeed anyway.

If you are honest and sincere, people may deceive you.
Be honest and sincere anyway.

What you spend years creating, others could destroy overnight.
Create anyway.

If you find serenity and happiness, some may be jealous.
Be happy anyway.

The good you do today will often be forgotten.
Do good anyway.

Give the best you have, and it will never be enough.
Give your best anyway.

In the final analysis, it is between you and God. It was never between you and them anyway."

– Attributed to Mother Teresa

When you were born, you cried and the world rejoiced. Live your life so that when you die, the world cries and you rejoice.

Cherokee Proverb

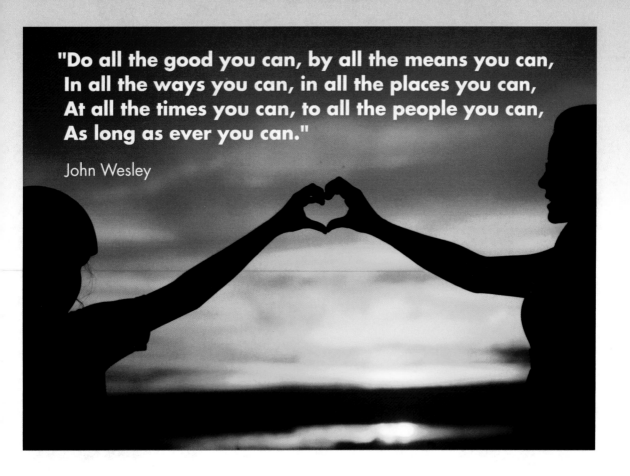

"Do all the good you can, by all the means you can,
In all the ways you can, in all the places you can,
At all the times you can, to all the people you can,
As long as ever you can."

John Wesley

"I sincerely believe that there is nothing truly great in any man or woman except their character, their willingness to move beyond the realm of self and into a greater realm of selflessness. Giving back is the ultimate talent in life. That is the greatest trophy on my mantel."

– Ozzie Smith, Hall of Fame Baseball Player

"Think of life as a terminal illness, because if you do, you will live it with joy and passion, as it ought to be lived."

– Anna Quindlen, American author

"Earlier in my life, I thought the things that mattered were the things that you could see, like your car, your house, your wealth, your property, your office. But as I've grown older, I've become convinced that the things that matter most are the things that you can't see—the love you share with others, your inner purpose, your comfort with who you are."

– President Jimmy Carter

Bonus Question

During my second month of nursing school, our professor gave us a pop quiz. I was a conscientious student and had breezed through the questions, until I read the last one:

What is the first name of the woman who cleans the school?

Surely this was some kind of joke. I had seen the cleaning woman several times. She was tall, dark-haired and in her 50s, but how would I know her name?

I handed in my paper, leaving the question blank. Before class ended, one student asked if the last question would count towards our quiz grade. Absolutely, said the professor. In your careers you will meet many people. All are significant. They deserve your attention and care, even if all you do is smile and say "hello."

I've never forgotten that lesson. I also learned her name. Dorothy.

– Joann C. Jones

An old Cherokee is teaching his grandson about life. "A fight is going on inside me," he said to the boy.

"It is a terrible fight and it is between two wolves. One is evil— he is anger, envy, sorrow, regret, greed, arrogance, self-pity, guilt, resentment, inferiority, lies, false pride, superiority, and ego." He continued, "The other is good—he is joy, peace, love, hope, serenity, humility, kindness, benevolence, empathy, generosity, truth, compassion, and faith. The same fight is going on inside you—and inside every other person, too."

The grandson thought about it for a minute and then asked his grandfather, "Which wolf will win?"

The old Cherokee simply replied, "The one you feed."

Legendary college football coach Paul "Bear" Bryant carried a poem around in his wallet titled, "A New Day" by Heartsill Wilson that reads:

"This is the beginning of a new day. God has given me this day to use as I will. I can waste it or use it for good. What I do today is very important because I am exchanging a day of my life for it. When tomorrow comes, this day will be gone forever, leaving something in its place I have traded for it. I want it to be gain, not loss—good, not evil. Success, not failure in order that I shall not forget the price I paid for it."

"I Wish You Bad Luck." Supreme Court Justice John Roberts' unconventional speech to his son's graduating class

"From time to time in the years to come, I hope you will be treated unfairly, so that you will come to know the value of justice. I hope that you will suffer betrayal because that will teach you the importance of loyalty. Sorry to say, but I hope you will be lonely from time to time so that you don't take friends for granted. I wish you bad luck, again, from time to time so that you will be conscious of the role of chance in life and understand that your success is not completely deserved and that the failure of others is not completely deserved either. And when you lose, as you will from time to time, I hope every now and then, your opponent will gloat over your failure. It is a way for you to understand the importance of sportsmanship. I hope you'll be ignored so you know the importance of listening to others, and I hope you will have just enough pain to learn compassion. Whether I wish these things or not, they're going to happen. And whether you benefit from them or not will depend upon your ability to see the message in your misfortunes."

"I'm starting with the man in the mirror.

I'm asking him to change his ways.

And no message could have been clearer,

If you want to make the world a better place.

Take a look at yourself, and then
make a change."

– *Man in the Mirror* recorded by Michael Jackson

"Why did it take an illness for me to recognize the value of time with him?

It seems we humans never learn. And so we relearn the lesson every generation and then want to rewrite epistles. We proselytize to our friends and shake them by the shoulders and tell them 'Seize the day! What matters is this moment!'

Most of us can't go back and make restitution. We can't do a thing about our should haves and our could haves."

— Cutting for Stone by Abraham Verghese

"If you want to change the world, go home and love your family."

Attributed to Mother Teresa

Excerpt from Stuart Scott's acceptance speech for the Jimmy V Perseverance Award at the 2014 ESPYs

"When you die, that does not mean you lose to cancer. You beat cancer by how you live, why you live and the manner in which you live."

– Stuart Scott, American sportscaster and victim of cancer

"It's sad that grandkids show up at the end of obituaries, way behind the list of work accomplishments, social clubs and survivors.

Why last? If you've got grandkids, you know they're first when it comes to the joy in your life."

– Regina Brett, American author

Three excerpts from Mitch Albom's book, *Tuesdays with Morrie: An Old Man, a Young Man, and Life's Greatest Lesson*

"Every day, have a little bird on your shoulder that asks, "Is today the day? Am I ready? Am I doing all I need to do? Am I being the person I want to be? Is today the day I die?"

*****

"These were people so hungry for love that they were accepting substitutes. They were embracing material things and expecting a sort of hug back. But it never works. You can't substitute material things for love or for gentleness or for tenderness or for a sense of comradeship."

*****

"As long as we can love each other, and remember the feeling of love we had, we can die without ever really going away. All the love you created is still there. All the memories are still there. You live on— in the hearts of everyone you have touched and nurtured while you were here."

"I believe that one of the most important things to learn in life is that you can make a difference in your community no matter who you are or where you live.

Do what you can to show you care about other people, and you will make our world a better place.

Kindness is the connection that links us all together and strengthens the bonds within our communities, neighborhoods and families.

There is clearly much left to be done, and whatever else we are going to do, we had better get on with it."

– Rosalynn Carter

Erma Bombeck was an American author who made people laugh and cry over everyday events. The following was written by Erma after she found out she had a fatal disease.

If I Had My Life To Live Over

by Erma Bombeck

If I had my life to live over, I would have talked less and listened more.

I would have invited friends over to dinner even if the carpet was stained and the sofa faded.

I would have eaten the popcorn in the 'good' living room and worried much less about the dirt when someone wanted to light a fire in the fireplace.

I would have taken the time to listen to my grandfather ramble about his youth.

I would never have insisted the car windows be rolled up on a summer day because my hair had just been teased and sprayed.

I would have burned the pink candle sculpted like a rose before it melted in storage.

I would have sat on the lawn with my children and not worried about grass stains.

I would have cried and laughed less while watching television—and more while watching life.

I would have shared more of the responsibility carried by my husband.

I would have gone to bed when I was sick instead of pretending the earth would go into a holding pattern if I weren't there for the day.

I would never have bought anything just because it was practical, wouldn't show soil or was guaranteed to last a lifetime.

Instead of wishing away nine months of pregnancy, I'd have cherished every moment and realized that the wonderment growing inside me was the only chance in life to assist God in a miracle.

When my kids kissed me impetuously, I would never have said, "Later. Now go get washed up for dinner."

There would have been more "I love you's"…More "I'm sorrys" …

But mostly, given another shot at life, I would seize every minute… look at it and really see it…live it…and never give it back.

"No matter what you've done for yourself or for humanity, if you can't look back on having given love and attention to your own family, what have you really accomplished?"

Lee Iacocca, American businessman

10 Ways to Be Remembered 100 Years from Now

We all want to be remembered—fondly—100 years from now. But the most promising path to that kind of immortality is via humility, nobility, self-sacrifice, and thinking of others. Have you taken the time to think about your legacy? Here are 10 ways to be remembered 100 years from now.

1. Don't live for your legacy – live for your family

Legacy building is counterproductive as an end to itself. People who value their family above their own ego tend to be remembered for generations.

2. Find your passion

Philosopher Howard Thurman said this: "Don't ask what the world needs. Ask what makes you come alive and go do it. Because what the world needs is people who have come alive."

3. Defer short-term gratification for long-term satisfaction

We work hard to teach this to our children; then we forget about the principle for ourselves! Is today's 62-inch TV really as important as your son's future education? Is the satisfaction of a well-timed volley of sarcasm worth the cost to relationships? Or is this one-night-stand a good substitute for a lifetime of commitment?

4. Build other people up

Ask this question, every day, "What can I do to encourage my wife, my kids, my co-workers, my friends…?"

5. Be an honorable person

What's better than money? Your reputation. What's more lasting than fame? Your integrity. What are future generations more likely to talk about than the coolness of the car you drove? The honor and nobility of the man who may well have taken a bus to work every day for all they know.

6. Define your life in terms of giving rather than taking

You don't have to be a rich philanthropist with your name on a wall to be remembered. Do what you can; give with all your heart. Lives defined by generosity make indelible marks on history.

7. Be authentic

Share your real self with your children; talk openly with your spouse; let your friends in. Men who build walls around their hearts and souls are not remembered – because nobody knows them. Tell the stories. How can we be remembered if we won't allow ourselves to be known?

8. Love your family

Does this sound like a no-brainer? Well, a lot of us could use a primer on love. Here's a quickie definition from the Bible that works—"*Love is patient, love is kind. It does not envy, it does not boast, it is not proud. It is not rude, it is not self-seeking, it is not easily angered, it keeps no record of wrongs. Love does not delight in evil but rejoices with the truth. It always protects, always trusts, always hopes, always perseveres.*"

9. Celebrate

Develop a culture of celebration in your family. Be like the family observing the 100th anniversary of great-grandparents coming to America, or the couple who exchange cards on the anniversary of their first date, their engagement, their first home closing, etc. Be the family that celebrates achievements, historical markers, memories, and anniversaries.

10. Find a wrong and right it

Maybe your great contribution is in process or yet to come. Become an advocate for what you believe in, and then allow your belief system to guide you into action. Socrates said that the unexamined life is not worth living. Maybe your legacy will emerge in response to self-examination and a long-term commitment to faith.

– Written by All Pro Dad

"I've learned that people will forget what you said, people will forget what you did, but people will never forget how you made them feel."

– Maya Angelou, American poet

Closed Book Quiz

1.) Name the five wealthiest people in the world

2.) Name the last three winners of the Miss America contest

3.) Name the last three Academy Award winners for Best Actor or Actress

4.) Name the last three Pulitzer Prize winners For Literature

5.) Name the last three Heisman Trophy winners

How did you do? Not too well?

The fact is that few of us remember yesterday's famous headliners. They're the best in their field but the applause eventually dies.

Now here's another quiz. See how you do on this one:

1.) List three teachers who aided your journey through school

2.) Name three friends who have helped you through a difficult time

3.) Name three people who have taught you something worthwhile

4.) Name three people who have helped you reach your goals

5.) Name three heroes whose stories have inspired you

Easier? The lesson is that the people who make a difference in your life aren't the ones with the most credentials, the most money, or the most awards. They're the ones who <u>showed</u> they cared and who have given much of themselves.

"Never lose sight of the fact that the most important yardstick of your success will be how you treat other people—your family, friends, and coworkers, and even strangers you meet along the way."

— Attributed to Barbara Bush, former First Lady

Things All Dads of Daughters Should Know

Being a dad to a daughter comes with a lot of expectations. This is one job that requires a lot of hard work and you need to cater to the fact that someone you love expects a lot from you. Here we take a look at some things that all dads of daughters should know in a bid to keep their daughters happy and to grow up to be women of good character.

Make Memories

Do not forget that your chief purpose around her is to make good memories. Give her a good impression of you; so that she remembers how good an individual you were and what a support it was to have you around in her life.

Teach Her to Live for Others

You need to keep reminding your little girl that it isn't always about her in life. She isn't the only person in the world and life for her extends beyond being selfish. She should give service to others and should realize the perks of it.

Go to Her Events

There is no bigger disservice to your daughter than not showing up in her events. Show up in her events and let her know that you are there in the audience. Your presence will only motivate her to do bigger and better things.

Do Things Together

Just the simple fact that you think you're there never means that you're always there. Proximity never equals presence. And, instead of just trying to be close to her, try doing things together with each other's presence in life.

Influence on Future Partner

They say that the kind of dad that a woman has, is the kind of person she looks for in her life. So, the kind of person you are around her is what she would be looking for from her husband going into the future.

Treat Her Mom Nicely

Although you should be treating your wife nicely regardless of whether you have a daughter or not, with a daughter in the home there is added responsibility on you to not go wrong here. Let her know that you love each other.

Be Emotionally Attached

Don't just shrink back as your daughters grow older. Be emotionally attached in their life and let them know that you're present through thick or thin and would be taking their side in whatever difficulty they face in life.

Date Her

Dating your daughter just does not mean that you should spend money on her. You should make your daughter realize how a real man would treat her girl. This would give her a fresh perspective towards life and more.

Value Her Heart

Her heart is really beautiful, so you've really got to admire that heart and give her recognition for being beside you. She loves you as much as you do her and she knows that you will always have her back no matter what happens.

Don't Blink

We will advise you against blinking, because shutting your eyes for even one second, will teleport you away from this role. This is a great time in life and you would never be able to experience euphoria comparable to having your daughter beside you.

"Shall we make a new rule of life? Always try to be a little kinder than is necessary."

J. M. Barrie,
Scottish novelist and playwright

"If that guy wants people to say nice things at his funeral, he had better pay an actor in advance.

One of the two attendees will be there just to make sure he is gone; the other one will be in dancing shoes."

– Old sayings

On the Day I Die

By John Pavlovitz

johnpavlovitz.com

On the day I die a lot will happen.

A lot will change.

The world will be busy.

On the day I die, all the important appointments I made will be left unattended.

The many plans I had yet to complete will remain forever undone.

The calendar that ruled so many of my days will now be irrelevant to me.

All the material things I so chased and guarded and treasured will be left in the hands of others to care for or to discard.

The words of my critics which so burdened me will cease to sting or capture anymore. They will be unable to touch me.

The arguments I believed I'd won here will not serve me or bring me any satisfaction or solace.

All my noisy incoming notifications and texts and calls will go unanswered. Their great urgency will be quieted.

My many nagging regrets will all be resigned to the past, where they should have always been anyway.

Every superficial worry about my body that I ever labored over; about my waistline or hairline or frown lines, will fade away.

My carefully crafted image, the one I worked so hard to shape for others here, will be left to them to complete anyway.

The sterling reputation I once struggled so greatly to maintain will be of little concern for me anymore.

All the small and large anxieties that stole sleep from me each night will be rendered powerless.

The deep and towering mysteries about life and death that so consumed my mind will finally be clarified in a way that they could never be before while I lived.

These things will certainly all be true on the day that I die.

Yet for as much as will happen on that day, one more thing that will happen.

On the day I die, the few people who really know and truly love me will grieve deeply.

They will feel a void.

They will feel cheated.

They will not feel ready.

They will feel as though a part of them has died as well.

And on that day, more than anything in the world they will want more time with me.

I know this from those I love and grieve over.

And so knowing this, while I am still alive I'll try to remember that my time with them is finite and fleeting and so very precious—and I'll do my best not to waste a second of it.

I'll try not to squander a priceless moment worrying about all the other things that will happen on the day I die, because many of those things are either not my concern or beyond my control.

Friends, those other things have an insidious way of keeping you from living even as you live; vying for your attention, competing for your affections.

They rob you of the joy of this unrepeatable, uncontainable, ever-evaporating Now with those who love you and want only to share it with you.

Don't miss the chance to dance with them while you can.

It's easy to waste so much daylight in the days before you die.

Don't let your life be stolen every day, by all that you've been led to believe matters, because on the day you die—the fact is that much of it simply won't.

Yes, you and I will die one day.

But before that day comes: let us live.

"Do more than belong: participate.
Do more than care: help.
Do more than believe: practice.
Do more than be fair: be kind.
Do more than forgive: forget.
Do more than dream: work."

– William Ward

Live your life for the next world and you'll get this one in the deal.

Live your life for this world only and you'll end up losing them both."

– C.S. Lewis

"Don't hate nobody." Ezra Hill, 109 years young, oldest living veteran in Maryland and second oldest in the country, when asked by Maryland governor about his secret to a long life.

"Always stay humble and kind…When the dreams you're dreaming come to you…When the work you put in is realized….Let yourself feel the pride but always stay humble and kind."

– Tim McGraw

Imagine one day you're in good health and then the next day you're told that you have only one week to live.

Would you rush out and try to mend the fences with people in your life that need to be mended? If the answer is yes, don't wait until it's too late. Act now.

– Stuart Clark, American author

Acts of Kindness

Every morning, a man places bird food in the yard for his wife to wake up to this view.

After a month in the hospital, a man was moved into a room where he could see out the window. His grandchildren wanted this to be the first thing he saw when he woke up.

This motorist stopped to help an elderly woman pass safely.

Every year, this kind man offers clothing, shoes and anything useful to anyone in need.

An elderly man had a heart attack while shoveling his driveway. Paramedics took him to the hospital, then returned to finish shoveling his driveway for him.

This retired gentleman, spent his evening making 50 tubs of curry for the homeless, every single night. Living on a pension and paying for this himself.

The Starfish Story: one step towards changing the world

Once upon a time, there was an old man who used to go to the ocean to do his writing. He had a habit of walking on the beach every morning before he began his work. Early one morning, he was walking along the shore after a big storm had passed and found the vast beach littered with starfish as far as the eye could see, stretching in both directions.

Off in the distance, the old man noticed a small boy approaching. As the boy walked, he paused every so often and as he grew closer, the man could see that he was occasionally bending down to pick up an object and throw it into the sea. The boy came closer still and the man called out, "Good morning! May I ask what it is that you are doing?"

The young boy paused, looked up, and replied "Throwing starfish into the ocean. The tide has washed them up onto the beach and they can't return to the sea by themselves. When the sun gets high, they will die, unless I throw them back into the water."

The old man replied, "But there must be tens of thousands of starfish on this beach. I'm afraid you won't really be able to make much of a difference."

The boy bent down, picked up yet another starfish and threw it as far as he could into the ocean. Then he turned, smiled and said, "It made a difference to that one!"

A middle school started a "Breakfast with Dads" program, but many dads couldn't make it and several students didn't have father figures. The school posted a Facebook request for 50 volunteer fathers... 600 fathers from all backgrounds showed up.

A husband and wife went out to dinner with their one-year-old child, and this is what was written on their check.

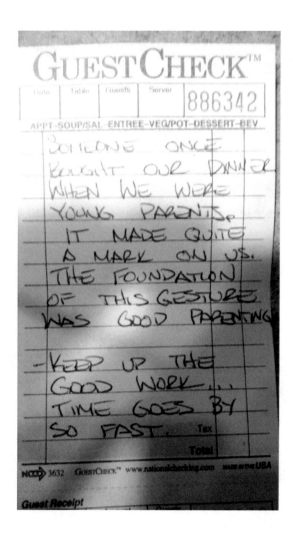

A Chicago resident posted the following message on social media.

Chicago, I need (10) volunteers to help me shovel for seniors tomorrow. I'm getting too many emails from elderly folks that need help. Meet me at the 79th St. Red Line stop at 10:00 am tomorrow. I got hoodies, hats and lunch for anybody that comes through.

65 people from 40 different communities showed up.

This woman made cookies and brought them to the local nursing home. The woman in the bed is Mrs. Posey. She was 112 and the nurse said she hadn't had a visitor in over three years.

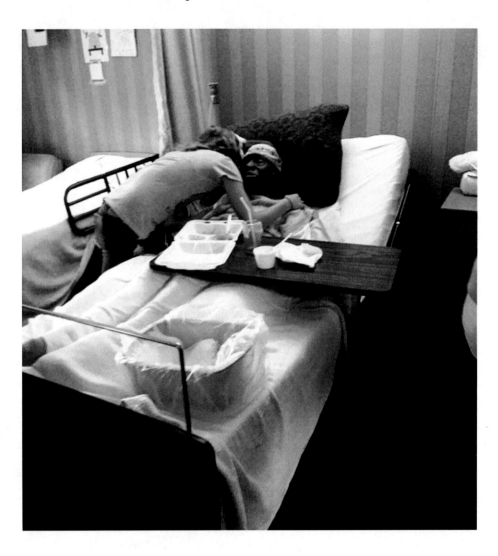

Every Wednesday and Thursday, this man goes to the local cancer centers and buys coffee for each patient, nurse, doctor and everyone in between.

This girl's father passed away when she was 16 years old from cancer. Before he died, he prepaid for flowers to be delivered to her every year on her birthday through her 21st birthday.

This man missed his train helping this older lady with her bags.

The bride's father died ten years before and his heart was donated. The man who received the transplant walked her down the aisle.

This tourist gave away his clothes to a man who needed them more than he did.

Thanking Our First Responders

First responders' duties bring them into harm's way every day. Police officers, firefighters and paramedics put themselves on the front lines of dangerous and traumatic events, and it's common to wonder how one can thank these individuals, perhaps lessening the emotional burden of their work.

Max Protzel, owner of a delicatessen in St. Louis, for many years had been giving a discount to first responders for meals at his deli.

A few years ago, Max and Jeff Drew met and decided to upgrade the first responder meal program at his deli. Jeff started an organization called "Thanking Our First Responders" and with the funds raised from his annual benefit golf tournament and from the generosity of many benefactors, they are now able to provide meals at Max's deli to first responders at no cost to them.

Max and Jeff estimate they serve between 750 to 1,000 free meals to first responders each year.

A Generosity of Spirit

By Rob White

When people do more than they have to, and do so with an attitude of generosity, they give of themselves in ways that lift all of humanity. The heart grows tender when we extend ourselves beyond what's expected. Going the extra mile is a vital ingredient that lifts our mood, allowing hopefulness to rule.

There are every day, ordinary, unassuming people everywhere who demonstrate the joy of offering assistance without expecting anything in return. They see giving as a blessing because of the enriching feeling they receive while lending a helping hand. The following are five examples of the acts those people perform, most of the time without even knowing it.

It feels invigorating to do something good for someone who can't possibly repay you.

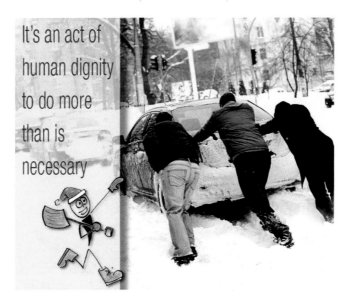

It's an act of human dignity to do more than is necessary

When you do a little extra, in the spirit of generosity, it never feels like it cost you anything.

Joyful living comes with the constant practice of doing a little extra

An act of kindness can heal even the deepest wounds.

A true act of compassion is to feel someone's pain,
and yet encourage him to keep going.

Gifts of love are not always packaged and saved for special days —
they are often given in the moment.

Spreading love
is often a
matter of giving
something
unexpectedly

The Cab Ride

By Kent Nerburn

There was a time in my life twenty years ago when I was driving a cab for a living. I was responding to a call from a small brick fourplex in a quiet part of town. I assumed I was being sent to pick up some partiers, or someone who had just had a fight with a lover, or someone going off to an early shift at some factory for the industrial part of town.

I walked to the door and knocked.

"Just a minute," answered a frail and elderly voice. I could hear the sound of something being dragged across the floor.

After a long pause, the door opened. A small woman somewhere in her 80s stood before me. She was wearing a print dress and a pillbox hat with a veil pinned on it, like you might see in a costume shop or a Goodwill store or in a 1940s movie. By her side was a small nylon suitcase. The sound had been her dragging it across the floor.

The apartment looked as if no one had lived in it for years. All the furniture was covered with sheets. There were no clocks on the walls, no knickknacks or utensils on the counters. In the corner was a cardboard box filled with photos and glassware.

"Would you carry my bag out to the car?" she said. "I'd like a few moments alone. Then, if you could come back and help me? I'm not very strong." I took the suitcase to the cab, then returned to assist the woman. She took my arm, and we walked slowly toward the curb. She kept thanking me for my kindness.

"It's nothing," I told her. "I just try to treat my passengers the way I would want my mother treated." "Oh, you're such a good boy," she said. Her praise and appreciation were almost embarrassing.

When we got in the cab, she gave me an address, then asked, "Could you drive through downtown?" "It's not the shortest way," I answered. "Oh, I don't mind," she said. "I'm in no hurry. I'm on my way to a hospice."

I looked in the rearview mirror. Her eyes were glistening.

"I don't have any family left," she continued. "The doctor says I should go there. He says I don't have very long."

I quietly reached over and shut off the meter. "What route would you like me to go?" I asked.

For the next two hours we drove through the city. She showed me the building where she had once worked as an elevator operator. We drove through the neighborhood where she and her husband had lived when they had first been married. She had me pull up in front of a furniture warehouse that had once been a ballroom where she had gone dancing as a girl. Sometimes she would have me slow in front of a particular building or corner and would sit staring into the darkness, saying nothing.

As the first hint of sun was creasing the horizon, she suddenly said, "I'm tired. Let's go now."

We drove in silence to the address she had given me. It was a low building, like a small convalescent home, with a driveway that passed under a portico. Two orderlies came out to the cab as soon as we pulled up. Without waiting for me, they opened the door and began assisting the woman. They were solicitous and intent, watching her every move. They must have been expecting her; perhaps she had phoned them right before we left.

I opened the trunk and took the small suitcase up to the door. The woman was already seated in a wheelchair. "How much do I owe you?" she asked, reaching into her purse. "Nothing," I said.

"You have to make a living," she answered. "There are other passengers," I responded.

Almost without thinking, I bent and gave her a hug. She held on to me tightly. "You gave an old woman a little moment of joy," she said. "Thank you."

There was nothing more to say. I squeezed her hand once, then walked out into the dim morning light. Behind me, I could hear the door shut. It was the sound of the closing of a life.

I did not pick up any more passengers that shift. I drove aimlessly, lost in thought. For the remainder of that day, I could hardly talk.

What if that woman had gotten an angry driver, or one who was impatient to end his shift? What if I had refused to take the run, or had honked once, then driven away? What if I had been in a foul mood and had refused to engage the woman in conversation? How many other moments like that had I missed or failed to grasp?

We are so conditioned to think that our lives revolve around great moments. But great moments often catch us unawares. When that woman hugged me and said that I had brought her a moment of joy, it was possible to believe that I had been placed on earth for the sole purpose of providing her with that last ride.

I do not think that I have ever done anything in my life that was any more important.

Lives Well Lived

Tony Snow, news anchor, White House press secretary

Excerpts from President George W. Bush's Eulogy for Tony Snow

Tony Snow was a man of uncommon decency and compassion. He was a devoted husband, a proud and loving father, an adoring son, a beloved colleague and a wonderful role model and friend.

Tony Snow, the professional, is a hard act to follow. Tony Snow, the man, is simply irreplaceable. Everyone who worked with him quickly grew to love him. We will always remember his wry sense of humor and abundant goodness.

We remember Tony's thoughtfulness. No matter how busy he was, this was a man who put others first. He would go out of his way to ask about people's families. He would check in with friends whenever he heard they were ill. He'd reach out to others, sometimes strangers, who were struggling with cancer. Even when he was going through difficult chemotherapy sessions, he sent inspirational emails to a friend whose son was suffering from a serious illness.

Most of all, we remember Tony's love of his family. There was no doubt for Tony Snow that his family was first. When Jill reached a milestone birthday, Tony had a huge celebration. He later said that he and Jill danced that night as if they were teenagers. He said he was the most fortunate man in the world to have shared love like that. So, today, Jill, our hearts are with you, and we thank you for giving Tony such a special life.

For Robbie, Kendall, and Kristi, you are in our thoughts and prayers, as well. We thank you for sharing your dad with us. He talked about you all the time. He wanted nothing more than your happiness and success. You know, I used to call Tony on the weekends to get his advice. And invariably, I found him with you on the soccer field, or at a swim meet, or helping with your homework. He loved you a lot. Today I hope you know that we loved him a lot, too.

Excerpt from a son's eulogy for his father, Kaliste Saloom, Jr.

My father has been given credit with making a very positive impact on this community during the 99 years he lived and was very fortunate to have received numerous accolades and awards for his contribution. Throughout my father's career he was also recognized as a champion for the poor and disadvantaged.

As a young man, I recall being introduced to a well-known leader in our state. The gentleman, who stood well over 6 feet tall, put his hand on my shoulder and said to me, "Don't let your dad's height fool you (my dad was only 5'4" tall). Everyone who knows him looks up to him."

Photo by Walt Seng. Courtesy of The Fred Rogers Company.

When speaking at public events, Fred Rogers frequently would ask the men and women in the audience to pause and remember an adult who showed them caring and kindness as a child. "Shut your eyes," he would say. "Remember that person. And thank them for what they did for you."

Everyone would do it. And when the eyes would reopen, most would not be dry. Fred could achieve intimacy when people least expected it.

Tonight, when I close my eyes, I will reflect as Fred asked us to, remembering someone who touched my soul.

I'm thinking of you, Mr. Rogers.

– Tim Reeves, American journalist

Tim Russert 1950-2008: A Good Life

By Alex Tresniowski

June 30, 2008

The Big Guy, as his son liked to call him, had to do something he hated—leave his family. On June 13 Tim Russert collapsed at work and died of a heart attack at the age of 58.

In the days after his collapse, those who loved him did something Russert would have loved—they told stories.

Sometimes Russert's generosity was small in scale. "I brought my 6-year-old daughter Ella into work after she had lost a front tooth, and he asked her, 'What did the tooth fairy bring you?'" says Fischer. "Ella told him $5, and Tim said, 'Well, the tooth fairy stopped by here too and left me another $5 for you.' I don't know who was smiling harder, Ella or Tim." Other times, Russert's humanity startled even his friends. "When my son Jeffrey had brain surgery about 10 years ago, Tim bought him a hat because he knew when you have brain surgery you need a hat," says pal Al Hunt of *Bloomberg News*, whose son is disabled. "Tim started this hat thing for my son, and now he has about 300 hats. Tim just cared so much about Jeffrey; he was the most reliable friend there is."

In the end, however, nothing mattered more to Russert than his family. "Before Luke was born, Tim made a promise with God that if his child was born healthy, he would attend Mass every week," says someone who often spoke with Russert about his strong Catholic faith. (Russert, who studied under Jesuits at Ohio's John Carroll University, always carried a rosary with him.) And no matter how busy his schedule, he'd always attend Saturday's Mass at the Georgetown hospital chapel.

Russert also rarely missed any of his son's soccer or football games, attended Bruce Springsteen concerts with him and thought of him "as my wingman," as Russert once told PEOPLE. "There were no barriers between them," says Luke's friend Mike Greeley, 23. "You would go to their summer home and there was Mr. Russert, in shorts and T-shirt, grilling burgers and drinking Rolling Rocks. He and Luke were comfortable sharing anything. They showed us what you and your dad could be if you wanted to."

If anything has helped soften the blow, says Russert's wife, it's been the outpouring of sympathy for her husband. "I had no idea Tim meant so much to so many people he didn't even know," she says.

In 2019, Budweiser released a video tribute to NBA superstar, Dwyane Wade. It wasn't honoring his play on the court. It was honoring the random acts of kindness that he has shown to many people over the years.

To honor Dwyane in his final season, NBA stars have been swapping jerseys with him after games. In the tribute video, five more people wanted to gift Dwyane with different kinds of clothing to add to his collection that represent his larger impact.

Here is how that played out:

- When a fire destroyed a family's home right before Christmas, Dwyane took them on a shopping spree. The matriarch of that family presented him with a t-shirt.
- When a young man who idolized him died in a school shooting, Dwyane wrote his name on his shoe to bring attention to his memory and comfort his loved ones. That young man's sister presented Dwyane with the basketball jersey that the boy had worn in his last game.
- When he took the time to meet with kids growing up in tough circumstances, he inspired them to change the course of their future. A young man whose life had been changed by Dwyane's encouragement presented him with the blazer he wore to his job interview.
- When a young student couldn't afford college tuition, he provided her with a full scholarship. This student presented him with her graduation cap and gown.
- When Dwyane's mom went to prison, his continued belief in her is what helped her turn her life around. He then bought a church for his mom for her to serve others and to help a community in need. His mother presented him with the purple robe that he had once given her.

The video then shows these clothing items hanging proudly next to signed basketball jerseys from the NBA's biggest stars.

It's incredible to see the difference Dwyane Wade has made in people's lives by showing them that he cared. He did this in a few different ways, including by giving his time, money, and attention to people at low points in their lives. He showed people that they mattered, and it had a direct positive influence on their lives.

It makes you think of all the little ways you never know how you may impact someone's life or simply their day. Now, Dwayne Wade has millions of dollars and a huge platform, so he can change someone's life instantly. But what about the rest of us? How can we leave this place better than we found it?

It's easy to get so wrapped up in fixing your own life that you forget about helping others. And while it's important to put yourself first sometimes, it can be extremely rewarding to help others in whatever capacity you are able.

"The purpose of life is not to be happy. It is to be useful, to be honorable, to be compassionate, to have it make some difference that you have lived and lived well."

– Ralph Waldo Emerson

Excerpts from a Grandson's Eulogy for His Grandmother

Mary Foote of Harrison, Ohio, shared this heartfelt eulogy, which was delivered at the funeral of Vivian Rippy by Christopher Eckes, Mary's nephew and one of Vivian's grandsons.

It's the little things that seem to stand out the most—her rolled up Kleenexes, her colorful muumuus, her iced tea and fried chicken, the aroma of her kitchen or a "yoo-hoo" from the other side of the door letting you know it was all right to come in.

I'm sure everyone here has memories much like mine. They are good memories, something we'll always have to cherish. It isn't often in our lives that we come across someone so special that that person stays with you forever. Grandma was that kind of person.

The only way to get hurt in this life is to care. Grandma cared more than most, loved more than most and was made to suffer more than most because of just how much she cared.

The kind of love Grandma felt for us was a love without condition. She may not have approved of everything we did, may not have liked some of the decisions we made, but she didn't lecture, she didn't judge. She just kept loving us, letting us know that she was there and if we ever needed her, we could count on her to listen, to comfort, to help.

She lived a simple life. It didn't take much to make her happy—a phone call, a card, a visit or a kiss before saying good night. We were the most important people in the world to her. She lived to make our lives better and was proud of us.

To think that someone like her felt that way about us should make us all feel more than just a little good. We can never forget that there is a part of her in each of us, something that she gave to us and asked nothing for in return.

Money can be squandered and property ruined, but what we inherited from her cannot be damaged, destroyed or lost. It is permanent, and it keeps her from becoming just a wonderful memory. It allows her in so many ways to remain just as alive as always—alive through us.

There have been and will be times in our lives when situations arise where we'll want so much to talk to her, be with her or ask her just what we should do. I hope that, when those times come, we can begin to look to each other and find that part of her that she gave to each of us.

Maybe we can learn to lean on each other and rely on each other the way we always knew that we could with her. Maybe then she won't seem quite so far away.

So, for your wisdom, your humor, tenderness and compassion, your understanding, your patience and your love; thank you, Grandma. After you, Grandma, the mold was indeed broken. Thank you so much. I love you.

A Beloved Mail Carrier Retired and the Whole Neighborhood Turned Out to Say Goodbye

Floyd Martin was a mail carrier in Georgia from 1985 to 2019. For his final 20 years delivering mail, his route was downtown Marietta.

"He's really part of our family," says Sarah Bullington, a resident in the neighborhood. "He's just really special." Neighbors would invite him to dinner. On holidays, they would try to make sure that Mr. Floyd, as they called him, wasn't alone. They brought him gifts. "They were there for me," Martin said. And Floyd Martin was there for them. He celebrated a number of birthdays, births, sports victories and graduations with the people on his route.

So, when some of the neighbors learned Martin was planning to retire a couple of months ago, they knew they had to send him off in style. Around 500 people live on Martin's route, and the group decided to invite every single one of them to be part of the celebration. Mailboxes were decorated. Signs were made.

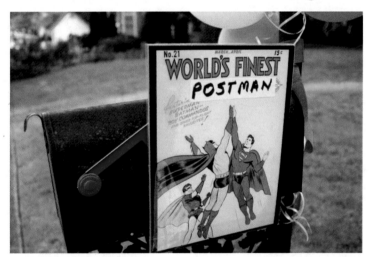

When Martin arrived on his final day, everyone erupted with cheers. "Brought me to tears, Martin said. It was estimated that about 350 people of all ages showed up.

"Continue to take care of each other," he told the crowd, "and smile when you think of me."

An Excerpt from a Eulogy to a Grandmother Given by her Granddaughter

Eighty-six years ago, God had a plan that through one life, over 130 more would be created, and hundreds beyond that would be touched forever. That life was my grandmother, Lois Domingue.

She was widowed while pregnant for her twelfth child and had only a high school diploma on which to fall back. Being thrust to the head of the household made her determination to provide for and raise her family stronger. She enrolled in the School of Nursing at USL and earned her nursing degree. She then worked at Lafayette General Hospital as a recovery room nurse until she retired over 20 years later.

She showed us love by establishing relationships with people from all walks of life, which enabled us to do the same. She showed generosity by taking in numerous people. In the Domingue home, one never really knew who might be at the dinner table or sleeping over for the night. Grandma offered shelter, food, clothing, school supplies, cars and even tuition to those in need. She helped people believe in themselves and gave them confidence—always generous to the point of depriving herself and giving freely without expectation of anything in return.

She was an entertainment director, mentor, cheerleader, motivator, listener, a mother, a sister, a friend. She was our rock—and so much more.

So remember and cherish your own priceless moments with Grandma Domingue—even if she did call you a name or two. Hold on to them and be sure to share those stories. In sharing, learn from her life—a strong legacy of faith, family, friends, and fun. One of strength, courage, determination, total selflessness, love, and laughter.

So, like she taught us, we have to look to the future and move forward. We must take her lead, making time for prayer and time for laughter. We must make her proud by doing kind works and being generous to others. We have to make each day count, live life to the fullest and to the best of our ability—each day as if it were our last.

These are only some of the ways we can honor her memory and celebrate her life. Find the ones that suit you best and do them. In this way she will live on through us and in our hearts, continuing to make a difference in this world.

Excerpts from the eulogy for high school teacher and football coach, Ron Holtman

I suspect we will all hear Ron talking to us for the rest of our lives. He did not just visit this world…he lived in it. And we and the world are much richer for it. He was one of those rare people who were a major character in so many lives…in so many life stories. Perhaps more importantly, he was a positive and pivotal life example for scores of young men for decades. For those who were taught by Ron or coached by Ron, he was larger than life.

He wanted those young men to have a sense of achievement, overcoming setbacks and hard-won success they could draw on later in life. And I don't think there was a single one of his former players who has not benefitted from the lessons that he so eloquently gave with a look, a talk or a nod of encouragement. He had a thousand ways of saying, "you can do it." Everyone wanted to do their best for Ron. Disappointing Ron was something that was unthinkable, not because there would be repercussions. You wanted to live up to what he thought you could be.

What struck me most about Ron was the breadth of his constituency. A lot of people have A-list friends and B-list friends. Ron had A-J. And there wasn't anyone he treated differently. Everyone he saw got the benefit of the light in his eye, a smile that said you were important to him and a good and honest conversation. His talk was seldom small.

When you look at the totality of Ron's life, you know words like honor, honesty, wisdom, integrity and humor all have real meaning. He embodied them all, and I will miss him.

– Harry Weber, friend and colleague

Randy Pausch, a computer science professor at Carnegie Mellon University, was dying of pancreatic cancer when he gave his fabled "Last Lecture" to students and visitors in 2007. The following are some excerpts from that lecture.

"You don't beat the grim reaper by living longer; you beat the grim reaper by living better."

"We cannot change the cards we are dealt, just how we play the hand."

"Just because you're in the driver seat, doesn't mean you have to run people over."

"I always liked telling my students: "Go out and do for others what somebody did for you."

"On April 11, 1945, my father's infantry company was attacked by German forces, and in the early stages of battle, heavy artillery fire led to eight casualties.

According to the citation: "With complete disregard for his own safety, Private Pausch leaped from a covered position and commenced treating the wounded men while shells continued to fall in the immediate vicinity. So successfully did this soldier administer medical attention that all the wounded were evacuated successfully."

In recognition of this, my dad, then twenty-two years old, was issued the Bronze Star for valor. In the fifty years my parents were married, in the thousands of conversations my dad had with me, it had just never come up. And so there I was, weeks after his death, getting another lesson from him about the meaning of sacrifice—and about the power of humility."

What does a hero look like? Not what you think

Ritchie Gibson

From his book *Be You. Be Great.*

Be the hero of your own story.

Having spent a quarter of my life in the army and having witnessed firsthand some of the most heroic men and women serving their country, I have always asked myself, "What does a hero look like?"

A great many of the people whom I served with and respect the opinion of would collectively reserve the term "hero" for select individuals. The term "hero" is defended for those who act in the face of danger or adversary while showing courage; they do what is morally right in spite of peer pressure. A hero is defined by his or her choices and actions, not by chance or circumstances that arise.

A hero can be brave and willing to sacrifice his or her life, but I think we all have a hero in us—someone who is unselfish and without want of reward, who is determined to help others.

My heroes are people like my family members, who have stood by me and supported me through thick and thin; my school teachers, who didn't give up on and believed in me although the time they invested didn't guarantee results; and a mentor, who led the way and took the time to steer me in the right direction when I was lost.

I've learned most heroes are ordinary people—it is their act that is extraordinary.

We all have a unique talent and skill set. What the world needs are heroes who have the ability to make extraordinary things happen in the environment we live in.

Performing an act of kindness or good deed, no matter how small, starts a shift of positive energy that can profoundly change lives. Doing something nice for someone with no ulterior motive can impact someone's life and give them hope for the future.

A good deed you did for someone today can have a far-reaching, powerful, and lasting effect on more than just you and that person.

How you affect others allows you to be the hero of your own story and sets an example of what is possible. You become an inspiration, opening the awareness of others to their own potential.

Think back to a time in your life when someone was a hero for you. I bet you have never forgotten what they did for you, their courage and their actions.

A hero is not necessarily someone who wears a cape, has superpowers and saves the world.

Being a hero is about helping others and endeavoring to make a difference in other people's lives, creating a ripple effect that all started with you.

Believe it or not, helping others is more about helping ourselves than about the people we are helping. We gain increased self-esteem, self-confidence and pride from knowing we are doing the right thing and making a difference.

Excerpts from eulogies for a father from his son and daughter

He loved BIG, and I'm not just talking about the infamous Hammy Davis bear hugs. You know, the ones that would suffocate you just a little. He loved big in the same way that he sang LOUD. He was vocal about his love for people, his love for his family and for this community.

A co-worker of my dad's said it best, "I'll spend the rest of my life living up to his example." Well Rex, I will too. My dad lived to build people up and give them any foundation he could to ensure their success.

Everyone was a friend whom he loved and admired in some way. One of my friends who would have breakfast at Edie's with my dad, like so many, said "He was genuinely interested in people and what they stood for." I think this is a cornerstone of friendship with Hammy that will be missed, he sought to understand what you really stood for.

I'd like to leave you with one final story about our dad that I think encapsulates my dad's song, or the "Hammy Way" and how he shared it with the world:

One week after my dad had purchased a brand-new truck, he was driving downtown and was walking into a meeting and a man pointed out he had a flat tire. He said he would be glad to help dad fix it. Dad, running late, always running late, handed over his keys to the man and went into his meeting. An hour later, his tire had been replaced and the man, who appeared to have needed the money, was gone.

Take this story, one story out of an abundance of stories about our dad and go on trusting others, giving them the benefit of the doubt and the opportunity to do good.

Know it will come back around, and if not, or if people let you down, "No Sweat". Carry this tune of Hammy with you wherever you go. Let us let him live and love through us. Give a part of Hammy to someone who needs a Hammy in their life.

Thank you all again for being here.

A few weeks ago, I attended the funeral of a man who had poured out his life into the lives of others. His passion was focused on helping organizations and Christian educational institutions provide excellence in the teaching of students. A tall man with a gentle smile, he would often be seen stooping down to meet the gaze of a 7-year-old, trying to figure out if going to school was ok. One Wednesday, as he was golfing, he was gripped with the pains of a heart-attack and went home to heaven.

David lived his life as if every day were his last. He loved deeply and served graciously. He talked gently and loved abundantly. In short, he made his life count.

What about your life? When the etchers chip your epitaph into the gravestone of your life, what will they write?

Many of us put wealth, status and power at the top of our list as indicators of success. In the grand scheme of the universe, these things are fleeting. So how can you live a life that is defined by true success? Here are 3 pointers.

1. ***Make it about others and not yourself.*** We are all born with glasses turned backward. We see ourselves as the center of the universe. But making your life count means to flip the glasses and put others first. Someone once said,

"The value of a man's life is in the counting of his positive influence on others."

2. ***Make it about giving and not getting.*** In our country, we have more than most people in the world. Health, wealth and resources more than provide a quality of life that most on the globe only dream of. Making your life count means filling the needs of those around you based on a heart of love. That kind of heart does not expect anything in return.

3. ***Make it about serving rather than self-seeking.*** Today, ask yourself, "How can I serve people around me?" "What is it that I can do for someone that is unexpected and will add value to their lives?" Even these simple questions can make people feel loved and, in return, you are fulfilled in serving.

If you seek to make your life count, you will have the kind of life that true success defines—please God by serving others. God even says that He sees what you do when you strive to make your life count.

Question: How else can you make your life count today?

Peace!

– Todd Stocker, American Author

Appendix

Volunteer and see remarkable outcomes.

Find the best volunteer opportunities in your area, go to:
volunteermatch.org

Here's another website with dozens of ideas of how you
can volunteer your time helping others.
https://www.dosomething.org/us/articles/community-service-
project-ideas

These sites match inspired people with inspiring causes.
It's how volunteers and nonprofits connect to achieve
remarkable outcomes.

Acknowledgments

Page 13

Still Foolin' 'Em: Where I've Been, Where I'm Going, and Where the Hell Are My Keys?

Author: Billy Crystal

Publisher: Henry Holt and Co.; First Edition (September 10, 2013)

Page 29

Man in the Mirror

Recorded by Michael Jackson

Written by Glen Ballard and Siedah Garrett

Man in the Mirror lyrics copyright Yellow Road Music

Page 30

Cutting For Stone

Author: Abraham Verghese

Publisher: Vintage; 1st edition (February 3, 2009)

Page 34

Tuesdays with Morrie: An Old Man, A Young Man, and Life's Greatest Lesson

Author: Mitch Albom

Publisher: Crown; Anniversary, Reprint edition (October 8, 2002)

Page 39

"10 Ways to Be Remembered 100 Years From Now"

All Pro Dad

All Pro Dad is a program of Family First

www.allprodad.com

Page 45

"Things All Dads of Daughters Should Know"

Justin Ricklefs

"15 Things Dads With Daughters Should Know"

Cole Damon, Culturehook

"Dads and Daughters: Here Are 15 Things Girls Need From Their Fathers"

Kay Casperson 30Seconds

Page 58

"Humble and Kind"

Released: January 20, 2016

Producer(s): Byron Gallimore; Tim McGraw⬚

Songwriter(s): Lori McKenna

Label: Big Machine

Page 114

"What Does a Hero Look Like? Not What You Think"

Ritchie Gibson

From his book *Be You. Be Great.*

About the Authors

Jeff, Stuart and Dave are childhood and lifelong friends who have always wanted to collaborate on a book. "We wanted to write something that is important to all three of us. We know our time on this Earth is limited and wanted to inspire people to live a life that will be lovingly remembered."

Jeff Drew is an award-winning international speaker who has presented hundreds of entertaining and humorous sales, service and leadership speeches.

He founded the "Thanking Our First Responders" program in St. Louis, Missouri and is expanding the program on a national level. This program partners with local businesses to provide free meals and many other free products and services to first responders.

Jeff is also a director of PGA Reach. PGA Reach is a charitable foundation of the PGA of America. Its mission is to positively impact the lives of youth, military and diverse populations through a number of programs and initiatives.

Growing up in Kirkwood, Missouri, Stuart and Dave Clark enjoyed an exciting childhood, sparking an artistic collaboration that has lasted a lifetime. They've had numerous creative ventures, including a successful line of humorous greeting cards sold through Recycled Paper Greetings called "Quote/Un-Quote." Stuart and Dave have also created two board games. "Out of Character" was their first game venture, and "Letter Rip" produced by University Games, is their latest. They have one previous book called **Funversations**.